Copyright © 2016 by Melissa Seamon-Johnson
All rights reserved. This book or any portion thereof
may not be reproduced or used in any manner whatsoever
without the express written permission of the publisher
except for the use of brief quotations in a book review.

Printed in the United States of America

First Printing, 2016

ISBN 978-0-578-18593-4

Dedication

I dedicate this book to my aunt Sheryl Johnson. Every accomplishment in ministry, I'll dedicate to you. I can never thank you enough for speaking life to me, at such a young age. I'll never understand what you seen in me as a child, but I pray I'm everything you envisioned. I still can't believe I'm here! There's not a moment that goes by that I don't laugh and say, "Auntie Sheryl said I'd be preaching one day." I just wish you were here to see that vision in fruition.

As I wrote this book, I remembered how you always reminded me how important it was to have a relationship with Christ. I've seen you hurt, stepped on, talked about, and betrayed in the church. There would be times you'd go in your car, right in the church's parking lot and just weep. I never understood why you would go back to church after all the pain.

You taught me a vital lesson at a very young age. You taught me that my main goal should be to please God and not man. You've always told me to establish my own relationship with Christ. As an adult, I've held onto those words. Your commitment to God have always inspired me, and I admired the way you've always managed to put God first.

Your love for God was evident, and you remained unashamed of your beliefs. Every day, I pray to God I could be on fire for Him like you were. I pray to touch as many souls as you did while you were here on this earth. I know if I stay focused on God, and His plan for my life, I can't go wrong.

I treasure every jewel you left me. I thank God for the times we've shared diving in the Bible and talking about what we've learned. I hope that you are well pleased with what I've accomplished thus far.

Love, Peanut

Acknowledgments

God, I'm indebted to you! I wouldn't be where I am, or who I am without you. Thank you for saving a girl like me. I love you!

To my beautiful mother, I only hope to make you proud. I only wish to be half of the woman you are. Thank you for being our superwoman. You surely do have an "S" on your chest. You're the best, and I love you!

To my Pastor Victoria, you are my divine connection. As soon as we connected, my life changed immediately. Thank you for pushing me to the next level, and thank you for walking with me every step of the way. I love you!

Abiola, thank you! From the very first day I told you I was writing a book, you made sure I worked on it every day. Because you had faith in me, I worked harder towards the completion of this book. Without your persistence, I wouldn't be here. I love you!

Stephanie Wade, thank you! I couldn't think of a better person to edit my book. Without hesitation, you came to the rescue. I'm honored to share such a special moment with you sis!

To my family and friends, I LOVE YOU!

Introduction

I want to start by saying, I had no idea I was writing this book. I was actually in the midst of writing another book before I realized I had a book ready to be published. God led me to write about some of my most recent experiences in my walk with Him. This book is not arranged in any specific order, but beautifully handpicked as I reflected upon each lesson I've learned thus far. As I began writing, I realized there was a need for this book. I was surrounded by so many people who experienced church hurt and walked away from God because of what they've witnessed in church. Many of my friends and family have been hurt by churches, ministries, pastors, or people in the church and they've lost all hope. This was my story too, but I thank God that I was healed from those past experiences. Now, my only desire is for you to learn from my experiences and grow from them. This book is for everyone who walked away from God, those who have experienced church hurt, and those of you praying for clarity regarding any of these matters. I pray that you receive insight, understanding, healing, and direction from my past experiences.

These lessons aren't talked about in a church setting. We don't get this in a new member's class, or Sunday school. We learn these lessons by going through them. Now, God has given me the courage to address some of these concerns. Not to "out" the church, but to make His people aware that things like this exist. I believe it's a common trick of the enemy, which is the devil, to continue to use this to turn God's people away from Him. Now that we're addressing these issues, we can no longer use them as an excuse to turn away from God. We now have the knowledge to handle each situation as it comes, and continue to have a healthy relationship with God.

With love, Mel

TREASURED LESSONS

Table of Contents

1. Give What You Have   Page 15

2. Mastering A Routine   Page 23

3. Loving Jesus   Page 29

4. Mentor or Hinder   Page 37

5. Spirit Mates   Page 43

6. Prayer Covenants   Page 49

7. Treasured Scriptures   Page 55

Give What You Have

When I first decided to give my life to God, I was under the impression that I'd feel an immediate change. I thought that everything I was dealing with would go away, but that wasn't true. In fact, when I woke up the next morning, I felt the same. I still looked the same, still spoke the same, and my surroundings were still the same. The only thing that changed was the fact that I gave my life to God, but that was it. To be honest, I didn't know where to start and I was all over the place. I did a little of praying, a little Bible reading, and attempted to fast but I still wasn't changing. I became frustrated because I knew I lived a sinful life and I needed to change, but I didn't know exactly how. So, I started working on my outer appearance first because I thought that would be the most noticeable change I could make. I wanted to change my hair, my clothes, and whatever else that I thought was sinful. I didn't go outside, I didn't converse with "unsaved" people, and I stayed in my house. I just wanted to please God with what I thought he was looking at, my works.

I focused so hard on trying not to say or do the wrong things and it almost felt like I was setting myself up for failure. How is it that the more I focused on not sinning, the more I sinned? One day, I remember thinking of what not to do and it was like God gently whispered, "Just give me what you got!" That stopped me right in my tracks! It totally made sense. Here I was, trying to change everything but God only wanted me to give Him what I had. You know, sometimes we make things so difficult, especially when it comes to God. This is what I heard, "Why are you trying to change yourself? Only I can do that! I like you just the way you are." You have no idea what that did for me. I instantly felt a sense of relief and decided to let God do the changing and not me.

I want to share a dream that I had. I will never forget this dream and I'll share it as long as I live. In this dream, I was a bride. My bridesmaids were so pretty and they were dressed in purple. I remember looking at their make-up, their hair, and looking at them in amazement because they looked stunning. I saw myself walking down the aisle but I could only see myself from behind. By the time I made it to the altar, I turned around and my hair and make-up was ruined. I was torn! I remember crying hysterically because I was the bride and two of the most important things to me were destroyed. I turned away from the altar and began walking towards my bridesmaids to be consoled. As they comforted me, Jesus came to me and wrapped his arm around me and said, "Don't be sad, I like you just the way you are." I remember looking at Him, of course he had no face or physical appearance. For some reason, I just knew it was Him. I looked at Him and my mascara was running down my face, and my hair was everywhere. I looked at Him and smiled and the dream ended.

We often times take advantage of dreams and what they mean. I do believe that sometimes, a dream is just a dream. However, I believe some dreams have a deeper meaning and this dream solidified my belief. In the dream, I was worried about my hair and make-up, which was my outer appearance. I was crying because I thought I was too ugly for my groom because my hair and make-up wasn't perfect. In reality, I was worried about my appearance. I struggled with the idea of God not accepting me because I was too 'ugly and sinful'. My dream was God's response to my prayers. I'd been praying about this for so long and God finally answered. This dream was right on time and it was definitely what I needed to move forward with my life. For years, my image haunted me and I finally was set free, through this dream. The dream was more significant than the obvious reasons stated. The Bible refers to God's children or God's church as the bride and it refers to Jesus as the bridegroom. God was telling me that I was His bride and even though I was a sinner, he wanted to have an intimate relationship with me, and was willing to take me as I am. Also, as I remember the color the bridesmaids were wearing, purple, which is symbolic for royalty. I considered myself to be a mess, but God saw me as royalty, and a part of His royal family. Isn't that something?! What a way to respond to a prayer! I didn't get this full interpretation at once, but as I shared the dream, each detail was revealed over time.

After I had that dream, I decided to serve God with what I had and to the best of my ability. I stopped focusing on my flaws and started to focus on my heart, and my desire to please God. When I began to focus more on God, I realized that I was evolving. The scriptures were transforming me inside and out. See, the scriptures reflected how sinful my heart was as opposed to my actions. Yes, my actions were sinful but I didn't just act the way that I did just because. I had an ugly heart!

That explained why I couldn't do right, because my heart wasn't right. As I began pursuing God and reading the scriptures, the word penetrated through my heart and exposed my sin. It revealed my heart, my thoughts, and these two things led to my actions. So, I was working backwards. I was trying to do right but the root of the issue was my heart. So even when I was doing right, somehow, I always ended back at square one. When you deal with the matters of the heart, you'll be amazed of how much you begin to notice. God works from the inside out, not the other way around. So, as my heart started to change, so did my thoughts and actions. Why? Because my heart was changed and the changes I made were now reflected on the outside.

Before I gave my life over to God, I wanted to be perfect and then give my life to God. In fact, I know so many people who try to get themselves together, and then give their lives to God. I use to say, "I'm going to change my life, but first, I need to stop doing this or I need to stop doing that." That's completely backwards! We come to God because we need a savior! We need someone to change us because we cannot change on our own. Trying to change with our own efforts causes us to put too much trust in ourselves, resulting in failure. Again, if we change what we do, it doesn't help us because there's a deeper issue as to why we do it. God reveals all! He reveals the deeper, the hidden, the covered, the deniable, and the things we overlook. He knows our strengths and he knows our weaknesses. We don't have to change for God to save us, we can come just as we are and God will accept us exactly how we come.

When I first came to God, I was still active in my old lifestyle. I was still battling, one foot in the church, and one foot out. I didn't have the power to change on my own because I wasn't strong enough and I was so accustomed to my life style. I was aware of my sinful lifestyle but I was afraid of change. I came up with so many excuses; I told God I didn't understand the Bible, I didn't like the members at the church, I didn't like my Pastor, and I even told God it was hard to follow Him. The more excuses I made, the further away I grew from the little desire I had to serve God. The fact that I didn't see an instant change caused me to go back to my old ways. At least I thought I was. I went back to what I knew or what I was most comfortable with. One day, I called up some friends and we had a session. A session is when a group of people come together and smoke marijuana and hangout. So, here I was at this session, talking with friends. All I remember is when I opened my mouth, nothing but the word of God came out. I began talking about the word, breaking down scriptures, and explaining what I was learning in the Bible. Everything I read was coming back to my recollection. I realized that I wasn't reading in vain but I actually understood it. The most interesting part about it was it touched those who were there as well. I noticed that they were in need of what I had and most importantly they needed the God I was talking about.

There was another time I was with a group of friends and we were in the car chugging down a fifth of Tequila. As we were about finished with the bottle, we were having random conversations and all of a sudden we started talking about God. One of my friend's father got in the car and I remember God telling me about his father. I tried to ignore it but God wanted me to tell him how anointed he was and how God hasn't forgot about him. I was so confused because I was thinking, "God, you do know I'm drinking, right? Do you trust me to tell this to somebody right now?" I still didn't say it, in fact I chugged the rest of the drink because at this point, I thought I had way too much to drink. God tugged on me again and I remember opening my mouth and BOOM, there I was talking to this man and telling him how God had so much planned for him. His response was, "Where did she come from? How does she know this?" Apparently, he came from a church and was well aware of what I was talking about because I didn't know him from a can of paint. My friends were so surprised and actually laughing because they had no idea I could talk like that, I had no idea I could talk like that. What God wanted to tell him was so urgent, that he had to use me exactly how I was to get His message across.

After that night, I had mixed emotions. I knew that was nobody but God that was able to deliver that message, through me, in the car but I also felt convicted. There was no way I should ever preach to someone with a fifth of Tequila in my hand and intoxicated. Although he knew the message was from God, I shouldn't have delivered the message that way. I repented for that but it also caused me to see that God was trying to get my attention. The signs became clearer that he wanted me to leave my lifestyle. I use to smoke a lot of marijuana, but anytime I fixed my mouth to inhale it, I would become paranoid. My episodes became so bad that I had to stop. I started disliking the club scene. Anytime I would go to the club, I would never enjoy it and it felt like I didn't fit in. So, eventually I stopped going out to the clubs. I also realized some of the "friends" weren't truly my friends. In fact, I only considered them friends because we had those things in common. I was changing right before my eyes. Although I was still dabbling here and there, my heart was changing.

I didn't stop everything cold turkey, some things were gradual and a bit harder to let go. It was truly a process but I was determined to give my best efforts. That meant I didn't hang with certain people, didn't go certain places, and I didn't do certain things. I tried to stay away from anything that would bring me back to my old habits and struggles. I knew I was on the right path because people started to notice that I was changing. They didn't quite know it was Jesus, if anything, they thought I was acting funny. That was my proof! The fact that they thought I was acting different proved that I'd changed. I wasn't looking for their validation, but because I didn't feel like I was changing, it was confirmation that I was. The more I read the Bible, the more my perspectives changed along with my heart, conversations and actions. I started seeing the results of having a relationship with God. My entire life changed and not only could I see it, I could finally feel it!

As I look back, I realized that God always had His hand on me, even on my worst days. I wasn't perfect back then and I'm not perfect now but God still has a plan for me. God was in the midst of it all and he never left my side. He was changing me then; I just didn't realize it. I was looking for drastic changes and instant results but that wasn't the way it happened for me. I'm the type of person who learns from experience because I'm hardheaded most of the time. So I had to mess up and go through some things, to really understand the depths of God. I know without a shadow of a doubt that I could've stopped doing some things cold turkey but truth is, I didn't want to. I wanted to do things my way and my disobedience delayed the process. I had to learn how to trust God each step of the way and that's how I was able to gradually change. We have to learn how to celebrate small victories! Often times we are so hard on ourselves that we don't celebrate the small changes that we've made. Nothing happens overnight and everything takes time!

Some people grew impatient with me and I totally understand their frustrations, but reality is, I had to change on my own. I listened to the counsel I received but it took time to process it. It took time for me to understand it and apply it. To change, you have to understand why you're changing and most importantly, you have to want to change. That's the beauty of change. We grow in stages and then we blossom into a butterfly. We have to be careful to not use that as an excuse or a crutch to continue to make mistakes. In our efforts, God will continue to meet us halfway. If he sees us constantly pursuing Him and trying to live right, he'll cover the areas that we lack. That's why God told me to give him what I had because he could take care of the rest. When I gave God what I had, he was able to bless it and make it good, and honorable to Him. I'm thankful for the patience God has with His children. If it were up to people, they would've counted me out a long time ago, but God said he still had a plan for me. Thank you Jesus!

It's so important not to judge people from where they are but to see them as God sees them. The Apostle Paul said in Romans chapter 10 that the people of Israel had a zeal for God but they lacked knowledge of God and His righteousness. I didn't understand who I was in God and I didn't understand His love for me. I loved God but I lacked knowledge because I didn't read or understand His word. The moment we get an understanding of what's in God's word, it's now our responsibility to act in faith. That means applying the word of God to our everyday lives and living out what the word of God says. We're also held at a different standard now that we understand the word of God. We're expected to continue to grow in our faith and continue to mature in Christ.

Again, I thank God for not giving up on me like many did! I thank God that I came back to Him because I realize many don't, so I'm forever grateful for His hand being -on my life. I want to encourage you to give God what you have and come back to Him. Don't look at your past or what you've done. I promise God is greater and has greater plans for you! Always remember that God is not a God of condemnation. That means in Christ we are free from the bondage of guilt. God doesn't hang your sin over your head, if anything; he wants to extend His forgiveness to you. So, give God what you have and let Him perfect it. It won't be over night and you may not even see the changes immediately, but know that God is doing it for you. All you have to do is give God what you have, and he'll take care of the rest.

Mastering A Routine

When I first gave my life to God, I remember reading the Bible all the time. I genuinely had a love for God and I enjoyed each book in the Bible. After I would read the Bible, I would usually pray right after, but I wasn't sure if I was doing it right. I knew that I was doing a good thing but I didn't know if there was a specific order, or if one went before the other or what. I became discouraged because I didn't know if my method was working or if God approved of the way I did things. It felt like I was all out place. One moment I'd be praying, next thing you know I was reading the Bible, and the next day I was fasting. I was aware of what to do but I had very little knowledge of how to do it. Now that I've matured, I realize there was nothing wrong with the way I did things. The only mistake I made was putting too much thought into if God approved or not. Of course he did!

I consulted with so many people regarding their relationships with God. I wanted to know if they had a special routine, or if they did anything different. Many were very helpful with sharing how they interacted with God. I was a bit intimidated because I met people who spent hours in prayer, or hours reading the Bible. I met people who were in church all the time and attended every revival. I began looking at my interactions with God and comparing them to what others did and figured I wasn't doing it right. I started practicing routines that I got from other people. I tried different prayers, different prayer methods, and different prayer times. I tried to read the Bible from the beginning and end, end to beginning, and it still didn't feel authentic. I went to church as often as I could and tried to be as involved as I could, but yet again, it didn't feel authentic.

I heard so many people talk about their relationship with God and how much of an experience it was. I became so jealous because when I would pray or read the Bible, I wouldn't have the same experiences as other people. I became discouraged. I thought maybe God was showing favoritism, or if I had to do the same things they did to experience God in the ways that they did. For a moment, I stopped. I thought that this whole Christian thing wasn't working and that it wasn't real. I remember saying to myself, "This thing is so hard, and everyone makes it sound so easy." No matter how challenging it was, something wouldn't let me stop. I picked up my Bible, and I started reading again. I began praying again, and I just wanted to try it just one last time, and who would've thought I'd be where I am today.

When you first become saved, there's so much that people throw at you. It's too much to understand all at once. You're giving your life to a person that you can't even see, that's challenging enough. People want to give you advice, they want to help you, but the truth is, it's overwhelming. As I mentioned, people have their own routines, their own schedules, and their own relationship with God. I think people make it harder than it actually is. When I became frustrated with "finding a routine" with God, God met me right where I was and led me. Let me just tell you, there is no specific routine! Sometimes, you may want to pray, other times you may want to read, but either way, God is pleased. As long as you're spending time with Him, I'm here to tell you God doesn't care which way you choose to start.

There are so many ways you can incorporate God in your day. Praying and reading are some of the most important ways you can fellowship with God, but it doesn't stop there. God is omnipresent, meaning God is present everywhere at the same time. You can communicate with Him in the car, at your job, at home, or anywhere you choose. God is going to always be there, no matter what. God likes to be the head of our lives in all that we do. He wants to be acknowledged every day, and in every way. Some of the ways I acknowledge God is just a simple thank you. I love telling God thank you randomly throughout the day. It gives me a chance to thank Him for all that he does. I speak to God on my way to and from work, which actually happens to my favorite form of communication with Him. Trust me, I know it sounds weird, but it's true. Usually during those car rides, I talk to God about my day. I bring Him all of my worries, struggles, fears, and the things that I wish to accomplish. Communicating with God in that way makes things a bit personal for me, and I always feel better after talking with Him. I always keep my

Bible with me, which is another way I spend time with Him. The way that I communicate with God may be different from the way you communicate with God, and that's OK. You'll develop your own routine over time that works best for you.

Mastering your own routine is very important. Your walk with Christ is intimate and between you and Him. In order to grow in your walk with God, you're going to need to give Him some of your time. For example, when you're dating someone, you're going to have to spend time with that person in order to get to know him or her. God is the same way. I remember when I was at a prayer conference and I asked, 'How do I have time to read the Bible, or pray?' This lady responded to me and said, "Make time." As simple as her answer was, it was the truth. I needed to make God a priority in my life and make time to spend with Him. Often times we let our schedules get in the way of our relationship with God. We become too busy for Him, and don't take the time to read and pray like we should. Some of us think that Sunday is enough time with God, so we only engage with Him once a week. I'm here to tell you, a day is not enough! We need God every day! He wants to spend time with you so that you can get to know Him. He wants to communicate with you in a way that's personal between the two of you.

God knows each of His children inside and out. He knows which form of communication is best for us. He knows how to get our attention and how to talk to us in a way that only we can understand. That's why it's so important not to base our relationship with God with God's relationship with someone else. All of our relationships are different but we serve the same God. Comparing your relationship with God to others will always distract you. It will no longer be authentic, but tailored by a relationship that he has with someone else. The relationship that you and God have is only for the two of you. He loves the time you spend with Him, and in time, as in any other relationship, your relationship with God will blossom. The more time you spend with Him, you'll began developing a routine, if one at all. You'll learn to incorporate God every day in every way.

The only right way to have a relationship with God, is to invite Him in your life. God has to have the invitation to be a part of your life. He doesn't want to be an unwanted guest. Reading the Bible, and prayer are ways to communicate and get to know God. Prayer is a two-way street. It allows us to talk to God, and in return allows God to talk to us. Most people don't realize that prayer is a time that God speaks to us too. If we ever have trouble hearing from God, we can always depend on the Bible to communicate God's will for our lives. The Bible has everything we'll ever need while we remain on this earth. If we don't use the tools God has given us, how will our relationship ever grow? It won't! We have simply just invited Him to our lives, and he's treated like an unwanted houseguest. If we don't communicate with God, we will never know Him and our relationship will never grow. If we do nothing else, we must master a routine of prayer and reading the Bible. After we've mastered a routine, we will make it a lifestyle more so than a routine.

Once you grow in God and understand who he is, it'll become easier to incorporate Him in your day. You'll understand that God doesn't only exist when you open your Bible, or when you pray, but he's everywhere. Remember, God lives inside of us. Wherever we go, God goes. That's the concept we must grip. Imagine having a friend with you all the time. Would you never talk to your friend? Of course not! This means we have access to God, at any given time. I mentioned previously, I love talking to God in my car. Can I see Him in my passenger's seat? No! But I know he's there because he lives on the inside of me. There are no restrictions on when or where you can communicate with God. My relationship with God isn't about how much time I spend reading the Bible but it's about allowing God to be a part of my everyday life. One morning I got up and decided to go to the pool. I was the only one in the pool that day so I decided to say a quick prayer. I was praying and I was moving my arms back and forth causing a ripple effect. As I moved my arms back and forth, I heard God say, "I'm making you as strong as a tide wave, and the ripples represent how rapid your words will reach my people." That was one of the times where I heard God clearly.

As you see, I was in an empty pool and I was able to talk and hear from God. I wasn't in a church service, I wasn't with a Pastor, and I wasn't necessarily trying to spend time with God. I incorporated God in my time at the pool by just saying a brief prayer of thanksgiving, and just by me doing that God spoke to me. When I spend time with God now, I do it anywhere. God knows how to speak to me in ways that only I understand. I like to think God does this so we can really understand Him and recognize His voice. When you take out time to really get to know God, His voice becomes clearer. I also want to clarify that most times God's voice isn't audible, but rather demonstrated by the things and people around us. God will use things around us to speak to us. God used the waves in the pool to speak to me, how awesome was that? I love His thoughtfulness and His specialty of meeting His children where they are.

So, now you're probably thinking of ways to start. Just simply start by telling God he is welcome in your life. Allowing God in your life permits Him to be a part of everything concerning you. Don't put too much thought into it. Ask God where he'd like for you to start, and if you're not sure, just start somewhere. You have to first know that God accepts the way you choose to spend time with Him. Once you know that, you'll be free to fellowship with God in the ways that you choose. No matter how you spend time with God, just make sure your heart is in the right place because that makes all of the difference. It doesn't matter if you spend one minute with God, just make sure to give God the best minute you have. Remember, God doesn't make us spend time with Him; it has to be something that we are willing to do. It's more enjoyable to want to spend time with God, rather than feeling like you have to. If you have to start off with a routine, that's fine. In the midst of your routine, it'll give you a solid foundation on what to do. Once you have your foundation down, you'll know how to incorporate God in your everyday life, and then it'll become a lifestyle.

It's going to take a little time to see the fruits of our routine. Often times, we don't know if it's "working" or not. I want to encourage you to keep going. Sometimes, the only way we can measure our growth is if we stay the course. Deciding to stay on the course simply means, walking it out. In due time, you'll see the difference that your fellowship with God is making in your life. When I first started incorporating God in my life, I spent thirty minutes with God. In that time, I prayed, and read the Bible. Over time, I desired to know more about God, so I increased my time with Him. Although there are no real time suggestions on spending time with God, I will say, the more you put in, the more you'll get out of it. The more time you spend with God, the more you will mature. I want to be honest with you, it took some time for me to gain the relationship I have with God now. The little thirty minutes that I spared wasn't enough. I started seeking God on a consistent basis, and then it was almost like a light bulb went off. As I spent more time with God, I became a reflection of Him. It changed everything around me because I was constantly seeking to be more and more like God. When God sees persistence, he rewards it by revealing Himself to us.

We all will start somewhere. Your main desire should always be to get to know God more than you did yesterday. God will lead you on how to spend time with Him but we must first learn His voice. Then, we transition from a routine, to a lifestyle and ultimately to a lifestyle led by God. After a while, the Holy Spirit will guide you on how God wants to fellowship with you. The Holy Spirit is just God's spirit living in us. Every born again believer has the Holy Spirit living on the inside of them, it was given to us once we accepted Jesus Christ as our savior. The Holy Spirit will lead us in our time with God. The Holy Spirit brings clarity, revelation, understanding, and truth. Being led by the Holy Spirit will never steer us wrong, so it's important that we transition into a spiritually led lifestyle. Your time with God will change over time. In fact, everything will change over time. You won't always spend your time with Him the same way every day. It's ok to switch it up, and you'll be led like that often. Remember, same God, but many ways to worship Him. Never stop acknowledging God. He's an integral part of our lives and we need Him every day.

Loving Jesus

To this very day, I cannot tell you the first time I fell in love with Jesus. I've been in church since a little girl; on the Sunday school bus, praise teams, in children's choir, leading praise and worship, and speaking. I have always been involved in church and I enjoyed it. Maybe it was the way the preachers spoke so highly about it, or the way the songstress sung about Him. Maybe it was the way people lifted their hands in awe of His presence, or how they cried when they thought about His goodness. Whatever it was, it was undeniable and I fell in love with Him. It's almost like I was born with a love for Him, although my mother didn't have a personal relationship with Christ but that's what that love felt like. It felt like it wasn't an option but something that just came with my birthright.

At a very young age, I had knowledge of the spiritual world. I would have dreams, visions, and I knew very well the difference between good and evil. My late aunt Sheryl used to always tell me, "Melissa, you're a prophet and your words are very powerful. God speaks to you! You're going to preach the word of God to the world one day." I didn't fully understand what that meant as a young girl and I didn't pay her any mind. My aunt was not the only one who told me that, I heard it everywhere I went. Preachers would lay their hands on me and pray over my life. Many preachers would gravitate toward me and would take me under their wing to show me the ropes of ministry. I remember one time, a lady called me up to the altar and she spoke over my life. She said, "You need to sit in my seat because that's who you are! You'll be preaching the word of God." Again, I didn't take anything serious because I didn't quite know what that meant yet, but as I look back, I know that it was nothing but God.

I became active in ministry in every church I attended. My mother always expressed the importance of being involved in the church. At that time, my mother was a new believer and didn't have much experience in the whole "church scene", so we've experienced a lot over the years. When you first become a believer, there isn't a church manual you receive telling you the dos and don'ts or what to expect. It all comes with experience. When you think of God, you automatically think of good or perfection and how everyone is "so nice". As a new believer, we often times trust easier than we should. We're quick to get involved, join ministries, offer a hand, and make friendships. Let me just say, none of this is bad and I honestly encourage everyone to try the things I previously stated. However, I'll say do everything in wisdom.

My experiences with churches haven't always been the best, but I thank God for what I know now. Some of the things I've been through would cause the average person to be done with church, as I once was before. I've encountered a lot of my hurt in the church. I've experienced manipulation, lies, gossip, betrayal, false doctrine, and a whole lot of judgment in all of the churches that I was a part of. As a young girl, there were many things I experienced that caused tremendous damage in my young Christian life and some I thought I'd never recover from.

One church that I was a part of, left a permanent mark on my heart but it was a wound God healed long ago. I was rebuked publicly in front of the entire congregation, at the tender age of 14. The Pastor at the time encouraged me to be a leader in the church. I led praise and worship, I spoke occasionally, I was a part of the choir, and participated in every youth event. She too reminded me that I would teach and preach one day. She always held me on a pedestal, and expected much out of me as a young girl. One day, she called me up to the altar full of anger. Apparently, she was told some second-hand information and from my assumption, a friend of mine in the church gave it to her. To this day, I haven't been able to confirm whether this was secondhand information or not but I wholeheartedly believe that it was. She told me how I was a sinner and how God was not pleased with me. She went on to say what I had been doing, and how I had been out to parties, hanging out late at the YMCA and how I'd better get it together before I went to hell. She said God told her all of this and he wanted me to repent for the things that I've done. As much as I believe in prophecy, and as much as I believe that God will reveal certain things to you, I know that God did not tell her that. It had to be secondhand information. I was nowhere near a saint, and in fact, she was right about everything but as I stated, this information was passed to her in confidentiality and was addressed publicly without the person's consent.

As a 14 year old girl, I remember being hurt that God was so angry with me. I didn't even care that she practically embarrassed me in front of the entire congregation, or the fact that the person who told her this information could've been a friend, but more so that I hurt the one I loved so much, which was God. Due to the fact that I was the lead in praise in worship, I could honestly understand her concerns. However, there was a way to address those concerns and what she did was totally out of order. Even after that horrific incident we didn't leave the church. We stayed around a bit but nothing changed and eventually, we left.

At another church I attended, I served as a receptionist and I was about 18 or 19 at the time. During this time of my life, I was not into church because of my past experiences. I was over the whole "church thing" but that undeniable love for Jesus was still there. My purpose for being in church this time was to receive a check, nothing more and nothing less. One particular day, a lady who attended the church and held a leadership position came to have a talk with me. She came into the office and looked at my tattoo on my leg and screamed, "Oh Lord! Why did you get that tattoo on your leg? Jesus! And you have a nose piercing? I think we should meet to talk to you guys about this." She went on to say we shouldn't get stuff like that done to our bodies and I remember her looking so disgusted with my tattoos and piercings. I felt so uncomfortable and immediately became offended with her delivery. It was almost like I was a disgrace. A few moments after her comments, we began talking about the Bible. I still loved the Bible and I was very knowledgeable about the Bible, despite the big tattoos I had on body and the ring I had in my nose. She was so intrigued by how much of the Bible I knew, and the fact that I could hold a conversation regarding Jesus and it being accurate. She said, "Oh my God, you are so knowledgeable about the Bible. I love that!" After that encounter, we established a relationship and talked all the time but she never apologized for judging me at the beginning.

Last but not least, there was another church that I was attending. I loved this church and my aunt was the reason why we attended. Her and her husband served faithfully in this church every Sunday. This church was very cliquish. There were several cliques in this church, so many that it was almost impossible to find where you fit in. There were many cliques, ranging from leadership, the praise and worship, the dance team, rappers, and so forth. It was a mess! It didn't matter what clique you were a part of, everyone was trying to get on the pastor's good side. Everyone wanted to be friends with the pastors. They brought all types of gifts and did all kinds of favors. Everyone was in competition with each other. As a church we should've been united but we were divided in every way. It was so much gossip, back-biting, slander, and confusion. It was so bad; it got most of our attention off God. It showed in our worship time, at events, and at church services. My mother got so tired of attending this church. My mother was so hungry for God and wanted to change so badly but because of the drama, it pushed her away from the church. It pushed us away from the church.

This is not even half of my experiences in the church. I've seen the good, the bad, the ugly, and when I say ugly, I mean ugly! I hated church and I made a vow to never go to church again. I stopped going to church for 5 years. I remember telling my late auntie I'd never go back because I can't stand the people. They were full of religion, judgmental, hard to please, fake, liars, and they were all hypocrites. That's honestly how I felt about church. Although I stopped going to church for a while, I still had that undeniable love for Jesus. I couldn't stand His people, but I still loved Him. I studied my Bible and prayed often. It wasn't as often as it should've been but I did it. I treasured that time and I enjoyed talking to God. The more I studied my Bible, I realized how some of the churches I visited didn't reflect the true essence of Jesus Christ. I wouldn't have known that if I'd never opened my Bible. This is why it's so important to know God for yourself.

As I stated, I don't regret going to any of those churches. It was truly a learning experience and I met some great people along the way. The truth of the matter is, there is no such thing as a perfect church! We all are imperfect people trying to please God the best way we understand how. There are going to be churches you visit where you'll experience a little bit of everything. Is it the way God intended His church to be? No! But it's just the way it is when you're dealing with imperfect people. We all make mistakes. At least 99.9% of people I've come across left a church because of the people! Not necessarily because of the pastor, but because of the people and the ministries they were a part of. I have no explanation as to why people are the way they are but you just have to understand who you are, and know that you have a purpose in God's kingdom too.

People are very fickle! We don't always find consistency when we're dealing with people. I'll use myself as an example. There are times when I'm energized, bubbly, goofy, friendly, and talkative. Many people know that side of me because that's who I am majority of the time. However, there's a side of me that's serious, observant, quiet, reserved, calm, and not so open to meeting people. It's just the way I am and have always been. I wish there was more consistency, but just like everyone else, we all have our days. That's how it is in the church. Let's be honest, we are coming to church after fighting all week long. We've endured so much throughout the week that when we finally make it to church, we are worn out and in dire need of God. We might need an extra boost of God. Some are fighting at home, lost their jobs, or lost a family member, getting a divorce, homeless, or going through a tragedy. We are all going through something and going to church to hear from God. You will meet all kinds of people, with all kinds of attitudes and with all kinds of mess, but don't let that stop you from going to church!

Pastors are people too! We often forget that. We look to them, in the pulpit and for some reason we think they have it easy. Truth is, they actually have it the hardest. I'm no pastor, but as a minister and being connected to pastors, I know for a fact that it's hard. Even as a minister, being chosen to lead God's people is a great task to begin with. Leaders have to lead people while going through family problems and pushing through their hurt and pain. In the midst of their own issues, they have to show attention to thousands of members, pray for families, spend countless hours away from home and most importantly, they have to be strong for their church and people who are under their leadership. That's not even half of what they go through, I didn't even scratch the surface. Sometimes, they don't have the best of attitudes. Sometimes, they don't have time to talk and they may come off unapproachable, or anti-social. Many people have had bad experiences with pastors or people in leadership and I'm not trying to make excuses for them. What I'm saying is, I know they need to improve, I know they need to get some things together, and I know they need to change. But still, don't let that stop you from going to church!

In the Bible, it tells us about our teachers, and those in leadership. The word never encouraged us to put our trust in man (man/woman) but to put our trust in God. When we go to church, we aren't going for the people but God. We should be going to church to serve God. We go to church to fellowship with God's people, praise and worship God, and to hear the word of God for encouragement. Church is actually a place to gather all of God's children and it was never made to be anything less than what it is. Unfortunately, people have used the church for their own selfish pursuits or desires, but trust me, God will hold them accountable for what they've done. Let God deal with them because you have to be accountable for yourself. You have to be so focused on God that you have no time to focus on the people. You want to make sure your relationship is right with God before you're concerned about a relationship with someone else. I say that because people go to church for all kinds of reasons and some may not have the same desire for God as you do. People will want you to gossip, people will have different perspectives, people are there to just hang out or are there because they have to be, etc. The point I'm trying to make is, everyone doesn't go to church because they have a desire to please God.

If you love Jesus and desire to get to know Him, don't let anyone rob you of that. I understand that you've been through a lot and seen a lot, but don't let them take away the precious gift of salvation. If I would've let my past experiences keep me out of church, I would never be where I am now. I started to find God on my own by reading His word. I got to know God for who he is and not by how people told me he was, there's a difference. Again, you have to know God for yourself. Once you know God for yourself, there's nothing anyone can do or say to change your love for God. Your love for God will help you deal with His children because after all, they are His children. They may not represent Him well, but we all are still His children. If you cling to God, God will show you how to handle these situations. You'll be able to treat people with the love of God even if they treat you wrong. You'll become an example of God's love and you'll shine light in those dark places. You'll be amazed at how your love can change a situation, and a person.

If you're currently searching for a church home or have some concerns about the church or ministry you're a part of, seek God. Lift your concerns before God and know that God will lead you in your decision-making. You may have some concerns about your leadership and if you do, go to God in prayer and address your concerns. There were many times I had concerns about leadership and I wish I went to God before I left the church. We as a people can be so hard on our church leaders. They say or do something wrong, and we leave. If we don't like something or if we feel offended, we leave and that's not right at all. Again, I'm not covering up the fact that some leaders are abusing the Gospel and manipulating the people but just because we had a bad experience, doesn't mean we should leave the church. Now, if something happens that doesn't sit right with you and is contrary to the Bible you read, you do have the right to bring it before God and if God tells you to leave, then leave. But don't base a person's character on a mistake or a bad day.

At the end of the day, we are all striving to be righteous and it's not always easy. Instead of talking about your brothers and sisters in Christ, pray for them. Remember that we all fall short! This doesn't give any of us an excuse but it's the truth. Demonstrate the love of God by how you treat people who mistreat you. You may be the reminder they need. Go to God on how to address it and deal with the situation. Do EVERYTHING with the spirit of love and understanding. Love is the greatest gift we have and I chose to love.

Mentor or Hinder

Starting out on my Christian journey was a very frightening yet exciting experience. I was excited to get to know God more but I was intimidated because I knew that it was a lot to learn and at the time, I wasn't in church. I studied a lot by myself and I would research different articles and scholars to help me understand what I was studying. I had so many thoughts and questions that I would discuss with my late aunt and aunties. I became fascinated with the Bible and the fact that I was establishing a growing relationship with God. My aunts were fascinated with me as well as I asked them millions of questions and addressed different scenarios with them. They were there every time I had a question or a concern, and they prayed with and for me.

I really didn't have a mentor at the time, so I studied the lives of others. I loved Pastor Kimberly Ray located in Matteson, IL and I loved Joyce Myers. I followed their ministries, their social media pages, their interviews, etc. I followed many leaders of the faith and even those who shared their testimonies on YouTube. I just wanted more of God and desired to learn as much as I could. I've learned so much from the people that I followed. I grew a lot from their teachings, but I also desired something more personal and to speak to someone on a one-on-one level about my growth. I was very patient with finding that someone because I didn't want to find just anyone. As I shared, my church experience wasn't always so great, so I wanted to be careful with who I confided in.

I was getting ready to relocate to Georgia and preparing for the move. My aunt Debra called me and said she wanted to connect me with a friend of hers to meet when I arrived to Georgia. At the time, this woman was a minister and an author. I thought that was kind of cool being that I wanted to get to know God more and that I've always wanted to write a book. We connected and she would invite me out to her gatherings. She'd always call me and answer any questions that I had She'd pray for me and she was always available for me. I didn't think we had much in common because she was older than me and she was in ministry. At the time, I was fresh out of my old lifestyle, so I was still rough around the edges. I didn't have it all together, but she still was there for me. That's something I would never forget because she understood that I was still learning. Most importantly, she knew that I was her assignment. She knew that God sent me to her.

Over the course of years, we spent a lot of time together. I'd spend the night over her house, we talked about God and prayed. I let my guards down and I felt comfortable enough to share some of my victories and some of my struggles with her. She instantly became a mother figure. She was very nurturing, loving, and caring. She treated me like her very own. We established a bond that was God ordained before we even realized it. She witnessed my growth as a person and in my walk with God. We started praying together once a week, every week. One day after prayer, she asked me if God spoke to me about becoming a minister. At that time, God had been dealing with me concerning ministry and I knew that I'd be preaching one day but I didn't know how. The funny thing about it was, I was getting ready to join a church but I never was able to. For some odd reason, I always missed new member's class. Once she approached me, I knew that it was nobody but God.

She immediately took me under her wing. Everything she knew, she wanted me to know. Everyone she knew, she wanted me to know. Everywhere she went, she wanted me to go. She loved pouring out everything she knew, so that I would be able to handle anything that came my way. She taught me how to study and how to do my research while I'm studying, and the list goes on. She knew where God was taking me and she wanted to make sure she did everything she could to make sure I was walking in my purpose. As I reflect on how far we've come, I can't help but thank God. Everything I aspire to be, she is. Everything I want to accomplish, she has and still conquering. This was no mistake; this was a complete set up! Thank God that it was a set up for greatness. Our relationship is still growing to this day. She's still right by my side, through the good, the bad, and the ugly!

I cannot express to you how thankful I am for her. I have heard many horror stories about mentors or spiritual coverings. I was close to missing out on this blessing but I thank God for His help. Before my mentor became my pastor, I supported different ministries. I was still trying to find that place where I belonged, so I was visiting different ministries for a while. I came across a ministry that I grew to love. I became active in that ministry, and started serving immediately. I took classes, preached, prayed, and even got involved in leadership. I was learning so much under the leadership there and the apostle over this ministry knew I had a call on my life. She said she wanted to teach me the ropes of ministry, she wanted to train me, and she wanted to make sure I walked in my purpose. I was growing in my gifts and she encouraged me to take more leadership roles. I was so excited because I had a place to use the gifts that God gave me and I had the support of everyone in the ministry.

I was thriving in this ministry and served as much as I possibly could. I received an offer to speak at a young adult conference. I was so excited at the time that I shared the news with the head of the ministry I was serving in. When I shared the good news, she was not as supportive as I thought she'd be. Her ministry was having something that same week and she really wanted me to be a part of it. As much as I wanted to, I felt led to go to the young adult conference I was invited to and I didn't think it would be a problem. She began questioning rather I was hearing from God, and if it was meant for me to go. She told me that God wanted to bless me at her conference and there were some things he wanted to do there. She told me that she supported my decision either way but didn't feel like that's where God wanted me to be. After our conversation, I didn't feel good about it. I automatically felt that she was upset with me and I was questioning myself. Did I hear from God? Is it meant for me to go? I continued praying about my decision, waiting for God to give me an answer.

Later that night, we met for prayer. On this specific night, it was three of us on the prayer line. Before prayer, she basically addressed the conversation we previously had on the phone openly. The other lady on the line had no idea about what or who she was talking about, but I did. My heart dropped to the floor because I couldn't believe she was responding to our conversation publically and during prayer. It went a little something like this, "People want God to use them but they're not ready. People want to speak and preach but don't want to go through the process." That's just a snippet of what it sounded it like. Trust me, I made it sound nicer than it did. I was serving in her ministry. I gave my time, my commitment, I was hands-on, and she knew that I valued her opinion. I looked up to her and really admired her work in ministry. What she did was not of God! It was out of selfish pursuit. Truth be told, God said it made no difference which conference I went to. Sometimes, people like to be so spiritual and this wasn't spiritual at all. All I needed to do was pick a conference to attend. It was that simple. That was just the icing on the cake. I saw some red flags and warnings previously, but because she was so well respected in ministry and very anointed, I ignored them. She was very possessive and territorial. She wanted everyone to help push her ministry, even if that meant neglecting the ministry God placed on the inside of you. Before I left, I had a conversation with her regarding how I felt. She took no accountability for what was said, in fact, she blamed everything on me and my emotions. I was hoping to rectify the situation and stick it out, but her lack of efforts and concerns caused me to leave the ministry.

That was another disappointment. When I was volunteering, praying, and involved in the ministry things were very good. But the moment I supported another vision, and put my time into other things, there was a problem. You have to be very careful when you see signs like this because it's not good. Again, she was well respected in ministry but a lot of women left this ministry because of the signs that I've mentioned. She wanted me under her wing, she made me feel special, and she mentored me. I relied heavily upon her because of her ability to hear from God, so I confided in her regarding my spiritual walk. She too knew the call that God placed on my life and encouraged me to exercise my gifts on her platform. From her statements, I guess she didn't feel like I was ready to go forth in ministry yet and I needed to sit under her a little bit more for experience. However, God thought otherwise.

We have to be careful with choosing mentors. If you're not careful with choosing a mentor you may end up with a mentor who will hinder you. Not all mentors have your best interest, believe it or not. Some of them turn out to be possessive, territorial, jealous, spiteful, and some of them like you to depend on them. They pretend as if they want you to prosper but they'll use what you have for their benefit. Some of them like to be treated like a God. They loved to be revered, uplifted, praised, acknowledged, and they love attention. They take advantage of your weaknesses and use them against you. Some could even hold you back from where God called you to be. The crazy part is, they are usually anointed and can hear from God! They know what God created you to be, they know you're anointed, they know you're destined for greatness, and they know your potential. If you get a mentor with impure motives, they will take what you have and try to profit from it.

You should never let your mentor take the place of God. God is the head of your life, not your mentor. If your mentor becomes your idol, you have it all wrong. Your mentor should always point you to God and not themselves. Their assignment is to walk alongside you but their ultimate goal is to see you accomplish all that God wants you to. They want to see you mature and grow in your gifts. A true mentor from God depends heavily upon God. They go to God for you, their prayers cover you, and they protect you. They never have to pressure you into anything because they know that God will have his way. They'll give their advice but they won't make you take it. They'll give you room to grow and they'll give you room to fail. They'll always encourage you to seek God and pray regarding any of your concerns because they know they don't have all of the answers. At the end of the day, they want to be sure that God is glorified in your life and they want to be sure that they're doing the best with the assignment God gave them.

When I connected with my God ordained mentor, everything shifted. I began walking in my purpose because she carried what I needed. As I stated, when I first met her she was a minister then she became a Pastor. Once she became a Pastor, she was able to license me as a minister. I was the first minister to be licensed under her newly launched ministry. She just started this ministry and I became the young adult director and a minister on staff. See how God set that up? She was chosen to help me walk in my purpose. Now, as I have my own ministry, she is alongside of me. We had no idea that our relationship would be what it is now but I know it was nobody but God.

As I previously mentioned, go to God before finding a mentor. Remember to be prayerful about every relationship, because although it may seem good, if God didn't send it, it can still be bad. People will offer to mentor you out of kindness and a good heart, but you still want to make sure God approves before connecting with a person. You can ask questions freely to whomever you choose, but don't be anxious to make a covenant with someone. Remember; never feel the need to rush into making a decision. Our God is the God of patience. He doesn't pressure us to do things and he doesn't manipulate us into doing things. He's gentle. Don't think that you're lacking because you don't have a mentor, it's not a requirement. I do believe it's beneficial to have someone to you can talk to regarding your walk. It doesn't have to be like mine, or anyone else's. If your relationship with your mentor pushes you towards Jesus, develops and matures you and you've recognized significant growth because of it, know that it's helping you. This doesn't mean you're tied to this person/s forever, but take what you can while you can, and when God says move, move. Know that you'll meet many who God will send to walk you through different seasons of your life.

Spirit Mates

When everything's going well, it feels like you're on top of the world. Your phone can't stop ringing, you can't pick between events to attend, and it seems like everyone wants a piece of you. It's a season of loudness, where you're distracted by the sounds of the world and everyone around you. And then, you go completely deaf, where you can't hear a thing.

When you reach a season where you have to go to trial, everyone scatters. The voices become faint, conversations become dry, people become distant, and just when you think people understand you, they don't. All of a sudden you're bombarded with memories because you remember a time when they needed you and you were there. But now, when it's your turn they're gone. You see, I struggled with this. I remember so many times when I would call people to pray them through, to pray, to speak the word, or even to see if there's anything I could do to help. I wouldn't let go of a person until I saw a breakthrough. I'm not saying this because I expect something in return, but I'm saying this because we've all been there before. We've all witnessed that feeling of getting the short end of the stick.

One day, I was driving in the car and I began to talk to the Lord about how I was feeling. Now, I believe God talks to us all in different ways and this is how God got my attention. I started to think about how alone I felt. How so many people knew what I was going through and how they didn't reach out to pray for me, or to see if I was OK. God said, "Now daughter, separate the people who aren't there for you and think about those who are here." I went down the list and I removed a chunk of people who I considered friends and focused on the few that I had in mind. Then God said, "Who's reaching out to you constantly? Who's constantly calling to pray for you? Who's constantly interceding for you? Who's constantly reminding you of my word? Who's constantly reminding you of who you are? Who's constantly reminding you of where you're going? Those are your friends who I've assigned to you in this season." My list became shorter and shorter. I was able to count my "friends" on one hand. As a matter of fact, three fingers.

At that moment, there was a wrestle with my flesh and spirit. My flesh wanted to personally give those so called friends a piece of my mind, while my spirit remained at peace. Whenever my spirit is at peace, it catches my attention. It's usually because God knows I'm going to say or do something that I regret. I resisted the urge and remained still, both hands on the wheel and God continued to speak to me. "Daughter, there is no need to become upset. I'm in control of all things. I've assigned these friends for you this season and removed the others. This season is very important and I have appointed certain people to walk with you this season." At this point, I was ALL in. God had my undivided attention and I was curious to hear more.

I'm going to share more about our conversation in a little bit, but I'm going to stop here to elaborate a little more on what God meant. There's going to be a season of your life where God is going to allow you to walk alone. I don't believe for one second we'll ever experience loneliness because the word says, God will never leave us nor forsake us but we will encounter a season where God removes people out of our lives. God is an intentional God. He created you with purpose in mind and he's assigned people to you, that will help you walk in your purpose. These people may not walk every season with you. You have people who are assigned to you for a season, a few seasons, or a lifetime. On the contrary, you'll have to walk with people in one season who aren't meant to go with you to the next season. Perhaps, their ill-intent or true colors might even be used to get you to the next season. Whoever or whatever it is, God is always mindful about who he places in our lives.

In order to grow, we must understand when the seasons are over and when friendships have served its purpose. Sometimes, we can entertain a person longer than God intended us to. The funny part is, we can feel the season coming to an end but we continue holding onto it, expecting it to thrive. The longer we hold onto it, the deadlier it gets, and the more it costs us. Yes, EVERTHING comes with a price and friendships can cost us too. God allowed me to see the people who were allowed to walk with me in this particular season. They each played a vital role and I needed them more than I realized.

I didn't realize how much I poured out. I would preach and teach, I would call people and pray for them. People could always count on me to pray them through a storm or advise them through a storm but I really never got anything in return. God was intentional. He knew what I needed and when I needed it! He sent me a young lady with a pure heart! She had a pure heart, pure motives, and most importantly, she really had the heart of God. By her having a heart of God, it was natural for her to care for his daughter. She witnessed how much I poured out, I prayed with her through some storms, I gave her Godly advice and encouraged her along the way. In return, she said, "Can I pray for you?"

Sometimes, all we need is someone to pray for us. I didn't want money and I didn't want sympathy, all I ever wanted was someone to pray for me. This is how I knew she was heaven sent, because that's all I wanted, someone to pray for me. I have no doubt that people pray for me in their own personal time but this was different. I was able to be vulnerable with her and trust her with my problems. Truth is, I was struggling with my own personal problems but I had to find the strength to encourage someone else. So God sent me someone who I could be real with. This person genuinely had a heart of God and had the love of God for me. She wanted nothing in return but just wanted to be a shoulder that I could cry on. God sent someone who could speak the word to me when I was spiritually dying and pray me through that tough time. She was full of love and God knew that's exactly what I needed at that time.

Another young lady came into my life, at the right place and at the right time. She too, was an angel here on earth. We instantly connected spiritually because it was totally a God thing! She reminded me where I was headed. She reminded me of who God called me to be, where He was taking me, and most importantly, that I was equipped for every good thing that was coming. I thank God for her! See, people didn't know I struggled for a long time with my calling. Some days I wanted to quit and she reminded me of who I am and where I was going. There was no jealousy or envy between us! She is a powerful, powerful young woman of God. I love the way she prays and the way she hears from God. God told me, "She's my daughter and she's here for you." We all walk in different callings and some are heavier than the others. She knew where God called me to, she knew the platform I was called to and she kept reminding me of the impact I am going to have on the world. No hidden motives, just pure love and angelic assistance for the assignment that was coming.

I call them my "spirit mates" because more than anything we were connected in the spirit. God handpicks your spirit mates for the assignment He gave you. This is so special because, I don't think I could've done a better job picking people to walk with me. God connected us and drew us to each other for something bigger than ourselves. Most of the things we had in common were spiritual! We had the same desire for God, getting to know God more, our prayer lives, and our loves for God. That was really the reason why God connected us, because we really had a love for God. Not just any love for God, but the love that God could use. He showed me that the love that we had for Him allowed Him to use us. When you love someone, you'll do whatever for them and that's the love we have for God. 'God we love you, use me for your glory.' I know many people have prayed that prayer, but we meant it and that's why God connected us, for His glory and to use us.

There were a few more who helped along the way, but these two stuck out to me! They were hands on and they walked this thing out with me. They are still here to this day, walking it out with me. I thank God every day for them. These two young ladies were focused strictly on the assignment. Yes, we had girl talk from time to time, and we enjoyed each other's company but we always ended it with prayer and with a fresh word from God. That's all the difference. Yes, you have friends who support you and are here for you but it's important to have people who can pray you through your assignment and push you closer to God, especially if that's your goal…getting closer to God!

I remember I was going through some things, and I called everyone in my phonebook looking for comfort. I found myself more messed up than I did going into the conversation. I was completely empty and all of the advice I got didn't help me. It wasn't because the advice wasn't good but most of the advice wasn't God. It was practical, and it made sense, but it just wasn't God. I needed people who could hear God because I couldn't. I was clouded with my own thoughts and moved by all kinds of emotions, so I couldn't hear God if I wanted to. The people who could hear from God knew when I was talking out of emotions, when I wasn't thinking straight, and they were always able to hear what I couldn't hear and see what I couldn't see. When I was receiving advice, it wasn't fulfilling because it wasn't God. It didn't make me feel better because it couldn't help me at the time. I was fighting, and I couldn't fight this battle with advice alone but I needed to be reminded of the word of God.

There are only a few people that God will allow to walk with you while you're on your journey. Your assignment is crucial to the kingdom of God and the cost is high. God invested a lot in you and he loves us so much, that he'll protect us by removing the people who are a threat to our destinies, or he'll allow us to see who's working against us so that we can make a conscious decision to walk away from them. Going back to the conversation between God and I that I shared earlier, the people who God sent knew my assignment. They felt the urge to call me and pray and remind me of my purpose. God put it on their hearts and I was their assignment in this season. God told them to cover me in prayer, sow into my life, and call to check on me. It was God! I'm so thankful that they were obedient and did what God told them to do.

Often times we become upset when we feel that people aren't here for us when they should be, especially if we consider them to be our friends. God will allow seasons where you can be acquainted with your friends but in the time of transition, and when God is getting ready to move you to another season, that will change. Some people will leave your side and some will stay. But God will send people to you to help you fulfill your assignment. I'll leave you with this, it's very important to ask God to guard your heart. It's not easy losing a friend or an associate and God understands that. That's why you can't be moved by your emotions because it'll leave you stuck and you'll never be able to move forward. You have to learn to become flexible with God because things are rapidly changing. People are constantly coming and going. But, God never changes! He's always the same! He's the same God yesterday, today, and forever more! That's one thing you can always count on.

I encourage you to pray for your spirit mates to come. Ask God to show you who's meant to walk with you in this season. If you feel that your friends are not able to help you, or you've outgrown some relationships, I can almost guarantee that your spirit is asking for more! Your flesh is thinking about loyalty, or the things that you guys have been through, and it supports the reason why this person is your friend. But, your spirit cannot find security in this relationship because this friendship isn't supporting your assignment, or pushing you closer to God. Your spirit will never be at ease! Just because your spirit mates are not here now, don't panic. When God is ready to send them, He will and you can trust that they'll be a help to you. Don't force relationships or scout for relationships. Relationships are very important in God's eyes, so remain patient. Your spirit mate has already been or will be revealed by you reading this chapter. They are on the way!

Prayer Covenants

When I was a young girl, I remember praying the Lord's Prayer every night before I would go to bed. I looked forward to saying this prayer every night. I loved praying because it was a personal telephone from earth to heaven. As I grew in my word, I began researching different prayers, how to pray, and what to pray. I grew excited and wanted to pray for everyone. I would call people and offer to pray with them or for them. I absolutely love to pray. I've spent years developing a lifestyle of prayer and understanding how to pray. I discovered that I had a greater passion to pray for people. I realized that people didn't know how to pray or what to pray and I was passionate about their prayers being heard. Not to say that their prayers weren't heard, but sometimes people feel better when they receive prayer versus actually praying.

I knew that prayer was one of my strengths. Like I said, I loved praying for people and will offer it to everyone if I could. I had all types of people calling me for prayer and questions regarding their spiritual life. I created relationships with people based on prayer. I had several individuals that I prayed with on a consistent basis. There were several groups that I was a part of and I was committed to each group. I know that God honors prayer. He loves when His children pray to Him and He loves when they intercede on behalf of others. I thought that I was pleasing God because I was connected to so many prayer groups and I thought God would honor the fact I was in them, but I was wrong,

One day, God told me to leave all of the prayer groups I was committed to at the time. I was at a loss for words because I thought prayer was such a good thing. God told me it wasn't the prayer that was the problem but it was the people that I was connected to. I remember praying with one of the groups and one person was praying their heart out. She was praying, crying, screaming, and shouting to God for a change. She truly had the heart of God and loved praying for others and I have no doubt her prayers were heard. God allowed me to see the others who were joined on the line. They had little to no faith, they came on the line because they made a commitment and not because they wanted to, some days they were up but most days they were down, and they had no spiritual stability. Although those things played a major role in the problem, God pointed out the fact that she poured out tremendously to this prayer group and when it was time to pray for her, she received the bare minimum.

I remember another time I was praying with a prayer group. I looked forward to praying with this group because I was really expecting God to do some mighty things with this group. So we prayed together all the time. We prayed for a few weeks and we started off on fire for God. As the weeks passed us by and we were headed towards that thirty-day mark, things changed. When I came on the line, my heart instantly felt heavy. There was so much doubt, so many complaints, so much negativity, and it truly became overwhelming. We put so much time in this group, we sacrificed our mornings and our nights to pray before God and it seemed like we were headed nowhere fast. I thank God for the people who were committed to this group. I know their hearts were in the right place, but the fire that we had for God, was slowly going out. God placed it on my heart that it was time to disconnect from this group, and all of the groups that I placed myself in.

When I walked away from the prayer groups, it was just God and me. I stayed committed to our prayer time and prayed for the groups that I left. I also prayed for those who truly had the heart of God and had the desire to pray for others. I prayed that God would lay it on their hearts to leave too. During my time with God, God showed me why I had to leave. That's why I love God so much! God will never leave you in the dark. If He doesn't tell you why then, he'll reveal to you in due time after you've learned your lesson. Have you ever got in trouble and your parents yelled at you for what you did but when things cooled down, they came back to explain to you why they had to yell at you? That's because after we've been chastised, more than likely we are ready to hear the why behind it. That's what God does. He waits until we are ready to hear the why behind it. God said, "Daughter, they don't want to be here, it's a routine. You're wasting your time." I remember thinking will I get in trouble for not praying for them? Isn't that what you said in your word? And immediately God said, "You can always call and pray for people, but don't make a prayer covenant with them."

A covenant is an agreement (i.e. contract, commitment, bond, promise, or pledge). When we agree to have a prayer partner, we are making covenant with them. We have entered a contract with them and like any contract, we have to stay committed to it or it's considered a breached contract. A breached contract is the failure to observe a law or in our case an agreement. If you breach your contract, you can get penalized, sued, and face jail time, so it's serious. The same way it is entering a prayer covenant. When you enter a prayer covenant with someone, the two of you come into agreement and you both have a role to play. In that time of prayer, you both (or all) have a responsibility to keep up your end of the agreement. If either of you don't, the other can be impacted by it. For example, you go out and get married to a person you've only known for a day. You agree to marry this person, coming into covenant with this person. As soon as you get married, you noticed this person is not who you thought they were. They began cheating, lying, not coming home, stopped working, and become lazy. This doesn't only affect them but it affects you too. Why? Because you're a part of the agreement and because the other person failed to keep up their end of the agreement, all of the weight falls on you.

Do you catch my drift here? If you're not careful of who you choose to enter prayer covenants with, all of the weight will fall on you and you can become ineffective because you will eventually get burned out. To go even deeper, entering a covenant or an agreement with someone, it means just that. You are coming into agreement with whatever they are in agreement with. A covenant binds you together and it makes you as one. If you don't know your prayer partner very well, I suggest you do your research. You always want to make sure that God approves of your covenant. God should be the one you seek before agreeing to be prayer partners with someone. You want to make sure this person is compatible with you. You also want to make sure this person loves God like you do, hears God like you do, pursues God like you do, and has the same zeal to pray like you do. As the Bible instructs, you must be equally yoked and that's in any relationship.

A prayer covenant is so important to have but with the right person. When you're connected with the right person, it's like heaven on earth! Being connected to the right person you will always be connected to God. God will make sure you both (or all) get the most out of your prayer time. Your prayer partner will carry what you need. They'll pray for you, war for you, cry with and for you, stand in the gap for you, encourage you, and most importantly, they'll take on your concerns like it's their own. It's so many benefits when you're yoked up with the right person. You can always let your guards down with them because you can trust them. They can make an intercession for you when you can't utter a word and they seek God for you. This person has your best interest! They will hold up their part of the covenant without a question because they know it's a God thing and since they're committed to God, they are committed to you.

When you are in a God approved covenant, you'll always see manifestation! God will always reveal Himself in your covenant because God honors covenants. Whenever you're in covenant with the right person(s), it will always bring out the best in you. If you're considering getting a prayer partner or if you currently have one, ask yourself are you bringing out the best in that person(s)? Are they bringing out the best in you? You should always evaluate how far you and your partner(s) have come to measure if this agreement is working for you or not. You have to see the fruit of this thing. This doesn't mean that if you don't see the car that you've been praying for in 6 months to kick your prayer partner to the curb. But how do you feel? Do you feel liberated, are you guys praying with the right motives, are you experiencing breakthroughs, are you growing, have you received revelation, are you stronger, are you wiser, has your prayer life developed, are things around you changing? This is how you can evaluate rather this covenant is working for you or not. Let me let you in on a secret: feeling liberated is always a sign that you're on the right track because God is freedom. However, if you're left feeling heavier than you did before prayer and you feel like the prayers aren't touching the ceiling. Use your discernment and seek God. I have felt that way before, and I found the nearest exit.

There are great joys and benefits being in the right covenant, but entering the wrong covenant is entering a danger zone. If you've realized you are in the wrong covenant, run for your life and I mean it. Being in the wrong covenant is literally death! One person will die and the other one will seriously be injured. I'm not talking about natural death but spiritual. Trust me, if you entered a bad covenant on fire for

God, your flames will be out by the time you leave. A bad covenant is draining! It does not leave you feeling liberated but heavy. When you're a part of a bad covenant, you'll feel tired, confused, helpless, hopeless, defeated, fearful, doubtful, uncertain, used, and you'll feel like God isn't with you. This person(s) is not committed to you. They cannot go to God on your behalf because they're too busy praying for themselves, and if they do pray for you, they don't have enough faith for you. They are always needy. They take, take, take, until there is nothing left of you. Their part of the agreement cannot be counted on because they are fickle, always in their emotions. Therefore, they're never in the right peace of mind to pray for you. They make their problems big and make yours seem small. Once again, evaluate the covenant. Ask yourself, is this you? Remember, you want to make sure you're holding up your part of the covenant and you can't do that by having any of these characteristics. Your partner(s) are depending on you, they need you, and they can't carry all of the weight on their own. Try to be the best you can be for the sake of them and their needs as well. A covenant is not one sided but two.

If you've realized that you may be in the wrong covenant, guess what? God will allow you to leave! He will not hold you back or let you be harmed by affiliation. Simply say your season is up and speak a blessing upon their lives. Let me tell you what you can do, you can still pray for them. Being in a bad covenant doesn't mean the person(s) are bad people. It's just we want to make sure that it was God ordained before we make a commitment with someone. So, instead of entering a covenant with them, just agree to pray for them and be there whenever they need you. Keep in mind, not everyone will be as strong as you are or mature as you are. Never leave a covenant relationship bitter or in malice. Some will get offended but that's OK. Your obedience belongs to God. Not everyone understands the importance of prayer and the severity of it. Understand that words shape your life and it's important to have the right person speaking the right words over your life. You have to be careful who you allow to speak over your life and who you share your life with. As much as I wish that we lived in a perfect world, filled with perfect people, we don't. We are all imperfect and I would give someone the same advice if they were in covenant with me. If you feel I am not adding to your life in anyway, leave and it's just that simple. I take covenant relationships seriously and you should too.

I highly encourage prayer covenants, they are needed! It's great to have someone who can pray for you and pray with you. Like I said earlier, God honors covenant relationships. Just like contracts, they can expire, so keep that in mind as well. When you enter a prayer covenant, it doesn't mean that that will be forever. Your prayer partner(s) will change eventually. Remember God knows what we are in need of and in every phase of our life, He'll usher in a person who's going to help us get to where we need to be. In the meantime, you be sure to be the best prayer partner you can be.

Treasured Scriptures

Here are some scriptures that helped me get through each of these treasured lessons. Each scripture gave me insight, direction, and understanding. Remember that we can find a scripture for every problem we'll ever face. If we respond to life's circumstances with scripture, the word guarantees success.

Loving Jesus

Luke 10:27
And he replied, "YOU SHALL LOVE THE LORD YOUR GOD WITH ALL YOUR HEART, AND WITH ALL YOUR SOUL, AND WITH ALL YOUR STRENGTH, AND WITH ALL YOUR MIND; AND YOUR NEIGHBOR AS YOURSELF." (AMP)

John 3:16
"For God so [greatly] loved *and* dearly prized the world, that He[even] gave His [One and] [L]only begotten Son, so that whoever believes *and* trusts in Him [as Savior] shall not perish, but have eternal life.(AMP)

Romans 5:8
For those who are *living* according to the flesh set their minds on the things of the flesh [which gratify the body], but those who are *living* according to the Spirit, [set their minds on] the things of the Spirit [His will and purpose]. (AMP)

1 John 4:9-11
By this the love of God was displayed in us, in that God has sent His [One and] only begotten Son [the One who is truly unique, the only One of His kind] into the world so that we might live through Him. ¹⁰ In this is love, not that we loved God, but that He loved us and sent His Son to be the propitiation [that is, the atoning sacrifice, and the satisfying offering] for our sins [fulfilling God's requirement for justice against sin and placating His wrath]. ¹¹ Beloved, if God so loved us [in this incredible way], we also ought to love one another. (AMP)

Proverbs 8:17
"I love those who love me;
And those who seek me early *and* diligently will find me. (AMP)

Using Discernment

Hosea 14:9
Whoever is [spiritually] wise, let Him understand these things;
Whoever is [spiritually] discerning *and* understanding, let Him know them.
For the ways of the LORD are right,
And the righteous will walk in them,
But transgressors will stumble *and* fall in them.

Matthew 7:16
By their fruit you will recognize them [that is, by their contrived doctrine and self-focus]. Do people pick grapes from thorn bushes or figs from thistles? (AMP)

Matthew 7:15
"Beware of the false prophets, [teachers] who come to you dressed as sheep [appearing gentle and innocent], but inwardly are ravenous wolves. (AMP)

2 Timothy 3:5
 holding to a form of [outward] godliness (religion), although they have denied its power [for their conduct nullifies their claim of faith]. Avoid such people *and* keep far away from them. (AMP)

Asking for God's help

Matthew 7:7
Ask *and* keep on asking and it will be given to you;
seek *and* keep on seeking and you will find; knock *and* keep on knocking and the door will be opened to you. (AMP)

Psalm 121:2
My help comes from the LORD,
Who made heaven and earth. (AMP)

James 1:5
If any of you lacks wisdom [to guide Him through a decision or circumstance], he is to ask of [our benevolent] God, who gives to everyone generously and without rebuke *or* blame, and it will be given to Him. (AMP)

Philippians 4:6-7
Do not be anxious *or* worried about anything, but in everything [every circumstance and situation] by prayer and petition with thanksgiving, continue to make your [specific] requests known to God. ⁷ And the peace of God [that peace which reassures the heart, that peace] which transcends all understanding, [that peace which] stands guard over your hearts and your minds in Christ Jesus [is yours]. (AMP)

Trusting God

Proverbs 3:5
Trust in *and* rely confidently on the LORD with all your heart
And do not rely on your own insight *or* understanding.

Proverbs 28:26
He who trusts confidently in his own heart is a [dull, thickheaded] fool,
But he who walks in [skillful and godly] wisdom will be rescued. (AMP)

Isaiah 12:2
"Behold, God, my salvation!
I will trust and not be afraid,
For the LORD GOD is my strength and song;
Yes, He has become my salvation." (AMP)

About the Author

Melissa has a passion to reach a lost generation. God began speaking to her at a young age, and gave her the charge to speak to His people. Melissa has always desired to teach people about God, and in August 2014, she decided to start her own Bible study. After seeing that there was a need for Bible study in her generation, she sought God to start something on a more consistent basis, and Lady in Waiting was created.

Lady in Waiting was a poem that Melissa read in the book, "Sabbath Songs", written by her Pastor Victoria L. Burse. At the time, she was in the midst of waiting on God to answer her prayers concerning the next steps in her life. The poem expressed the importance of waiting on God, and the rewards of waiting on Him. As Melissa sought after God concerning her life, He showed her what to do while waiting for Him, and encouraged her to share it with young women. Lady in Waiting started as a series, and was birthed into a ministry.

Melissa was licensed as a minister on November 21st, 2015, by the ARC International Ministries, in Riverdale, Georgia, where Victoria Burse serves as Pastor/Teacher. She serves as a minister on staff, and a chief intercessor. Melissa desires to grow into the woman God has called her to be. She continues to be a present voice in her generation. She loves to teach, and has a true heart for God's people.

"I desire to be all that God created me to be. I don't know what that is yet, but I pray that I'm able to receive whatever it is that He has. One thing we can be certain of, God cannot fail!"

For all booking inquiries, please e-mail: mseajohn@gmail.com
Visit @iamaladyinwaiting.com to stay connected with our ministry.

www.ingramcontent.com/pod-product-compliance
Lightning Source LLC
Chambersburg PA
CBHW032218040426
42449CB00005B/652